D1450154

AD 1250	ITALY	EUROPE

1250–1494 Italy is split up into many different states. Florence, Venice, and Milan gain in wealth and power

1248–1270 Seventh Crusade led by Louis IX of France

1306 Giotto completes series of frescoes in Padua
1307 Dante Alighieri begins to write the *Divine Comedy*

1341 Francesco Petrarch crowned Poet Laureate, Rome
1348 Black Death ravages Italy and the rest of Europe

1338 Beginning of Hundred Years' War (ends 1453)

1348 Black Death ravages Europe (until 1351)

1400

1397 Medici bank is founded in Florence
1402 Ghiberti wins competition for the Baptistery doors, Florence

1420 Brunelleschi begins to build his dome for Florence Cathedral

1415 Henry V of England invades France and defeats French at Agincourt

1431 Jeanne d'Arc burned as a witch

1454 Printing by movable type perfected in Germany by Johannes Gutenberg
1456 Turks capture Athens

1490 Aldus Manutius sets up Aldine press at Venice

1494–1559 France and Spain invade disunited Italy
1498 Savonarola burned at the stake

1492 Muslims expelled from Granada (Spain)

1500

1504 Michelangelo completes his statue of David

1517 Reformation begins: Martin Luther nails "protests" on church door at Wittenberg
1521 Diet of Worms: Martin Luther is condemned as a heretic and is excommunicated
1527 Sack of Rome by Holy Roman Emperor

1532 Religious Peace of Nuremberg: Protestants allowed to practice their religion freely
1559 Treaty of Cateau-Cambrésis. Habsburg Spain established as dominant power in Italy
1545 Pope Paul III opens the Council of Trent which is to reform the Roman Catholic Church

1559

NEAR EAST

ELSEWHERE

1260 Mamluk Turks control Egypt and
Syria
1291 Saracens (Muslims) capture Acre
from Christians
1301 Osman defeats Byzantines

1271–1275 Marco Polo, the Venetian
explorer, travels to Cathay (China)
1294 Death of Kublai Khan

1363 Timur the Lame begins
conquest of Asia
1368 Ming Dynasty in China (to 1644)

1379 Timur the Lame (Tamerlane)
invades Persia
1390 Turks conquer Asia Minor

1402 Timur the Lame completes
conquest of most of Ottoman empire

1421 Peking becomes capital of China

1451 Mehemmed II becomes Sultan of
Turkey

1453 Ottoman Turks capture
Constantinople (Byzantium): end of
the Byzantine empire and of the
Middle Ages
1472 Venetians destroy Smyrna
1475 Turks conquer Crimea

1455 West Africa explored by the
Venetian Cadamosto
1467 Start of civil wars in Japan

1492 Christopher Columbus discovers
the New World
1497 John Cabot discovers
Newfoundland
1498 Vasco da Gama of Portugal
reaches India
1501 Amerigo Vespucci explores coast
of Brazil
1513 Portuguese reach Canton, China

1517 Ottoman Turks capture Cairo;
end of Mamluk empire

1520 Suleiman the Magnificent of
Turkey begins 46-year reign

1522 First circumnavigation of the
world by Magellan's expedition
1526 Mughal empire founded

1549 St Francis Xavier introduces
Christianity to Japan

1554 Turks conquer coast of North
Africa

1557 Portuguese settle at Macao,
China

842914

Renaissance Italy

Warwick Press

Contents

Top: The poet Dante from a painting of 1465. Center: The dome of St. Peter's Rome, built in the 16th century, which Michelangelo helped to design. Below: The three Graces, from the "Primavera", painted by Botticelli in 1478. Previous page: A bronze panel cast by Ghiberti in 1402, showing an Old Testament scene of the prophet Abraham about to sacrifice his son Isaac.

Editorial

Author
Anton Powell

Editor
Frances M. Clapham

Assistant Editor
Elizabeth Wiltshire

Illustrators
Richard Hook
Roger Phillips

Published 1980 by Warwick Press, 730 Fifth Avenue, New York, New York 10019.

First published in Great Britain by Longman Group, Limited, 1979.

Copyright © 1979 by Grisewood & Dempsey Ltd.

Printed in Italy by New Interlitho, Milan.

6 5 4 3 2 1   All rights reserved.

Library of Congress Catalog Card No. 79-89729

ISBN 0-531-09164-3

Renaissance Italy

The word *Renaissance* means "rebirth". We use it to describe the rebirth of the knowledge of the Ancient Greeks and Romans which took place from the 13th to the early 17th centuries. Much of this knowledge had been lost after the Barbarians overthrew Roman rule in Europe in the 5th century AD. Roman laws and customs died out; Roman buildings crumbled away. Many of the books by Roman and Greek writers were lost. Only a few remained, often locked away in monastery libraries where they were never seen.

The Renaissance began in Italy, and spread from there to the rest of Europe. In this book we look at Italy during this period, and at the conditions there which led to the new interest in the old learning. We see how scholars, artists, and scientists used the old knowledge as the foundation for new ideas of their own. These new ideas were sometimes approved of by the Church, but could also be thought of as a threat to its teachings. Eventually they were to lead to changes in the Church itself. They also led to changes in the lives of ordinary people. And they are important now because they have helped to shape the way we live.

Above : Perseus, by the 16th-century sculptor Cellini. Perseus has just killed the female monster Medusa.
Below : The Gonzaga family, painted in the late 15th century by Mantegna. The Gonzagas were the ruling family of Mantua, and they were great patrons of the new Renaissance learning.

Setting the Scene

The wealth and independence of Italian city states encouraged a new interest in learning and art.

The wealthy trading city of Florence was one of the great centers of Renaissance learning and art. This view shows the cathedral which was begun in the late 13th century. The famous dome was built in the early 15th century by Brunelleschi.

Italy, from the 13th to the early 17th centuries, produced some of the most exciting developments in the history of mankind. We call this period the *Renaissance*, a word meaning "rebirth". It comes from the rebirth and rediscovery at this time of the knowledge which great thinkers of Ancient Greece and Rome had possessed. Before the Renaissance, in the period known as the Middle Ages (see page 43), the great works of Greece and Rome had been largely, though not entirely, forgotten. In this medieval period artists and thoughtful writers had been more interested in the Bible and religious subjects than in other areas of knowledge. Progress in other fields had been slow.

With the ending of the Middle Ages, men and women of the Renaissance perhaps came to think rather less often of heaven, and to take more pride and enjoyment in themselves and the world around them. They paid artists to paint their portraits against the beautiful Italian countryside. They also grew to believe that there was far more to be discovered about mankind and the world than medieval people had known. They were eager to rediscover what clever Greeks and Romans had known in ancient times. Like the Romans, Renaissance Italians began to have contacts with China. Like the Greeks, they learned to make lifelike sculptures, as well as making intelligent attempts to understand the world. This renewed interest in the world and in mankind is called *humanism*.

In many ways the discoveries of the Renaissance went far beyond those of the Greeks and Romans. It was a Renaissance Italian who discovered America. Doctors in Renaissance Italy were the first Europeans to understand how blood circulates in the body. They also gave a new and sensible explanation of infectious diseases. One scientist of the Renaissance invented the thermometer. Another made imaginative plans for tanks, explosive shells, and parachutes, centuries before other scientists put such inventions into practice.

We know a great deal today about rich people of this time – the dukes and generals, successful merchants, artists, and writers. But while they were enjoying the new ideas in art and science, the poor people in the towns and countryside often lived in dirt and misery. Far less is known about these people, who sailed the trading galleys, produced the food, and cut the stone for the fine buildings. But for almost everyone, rich or poor, life in the Italian Renaissance could be violent and dangerous.

CHRONOLOGY

1250–1494 Italy is split up into many different states. City states of northern and central Italy – Florence, Venice, and Milan – gain in wealth and power. Southern Italy remains poor and backward

1305 Papal See removed from Rome to Avignon

1306 Giotto completes series of frescoes in Padua

1307 Dante Alighieri begins to write the "Divine Comedy"

1341 Francesco Petrarch crowned Poet Laureate in Rome

1348 Black Death ravages Italy and the rest of Europe

1353 Giovanni Boccaccio finishes writing the "Decameron"

1378 The Great Schism: rival popes are elected – one in Rome and an antipope in Avignon

1397 Medici bank is founded in Florence

1402 Ghiberti wins competition for the Baptistery doors, Florence

1417 End of Great Schism: Martin V elected Pope in Rome

1420 Brunelleschi begins to build his dome for Florence Cathedral

1434 Cosimo de' Medici becomes ruler of Florence

1447 Pope Nicholas V founds the Vatican library

1450 Francesco Sforza conquers Milan

1463 Venice begins 16-year war with Ottoman Turks

1465 First printing press in Italy set up near Rome

1469 Lorenzo de' Medici becomes ruler of Florence

1479 Treaty of Constantinople: Venice agrees to pay tribute to the Ottoman empire for trading rights in Black Sea

1490 Aldus Manutius sets up Aldine press in Venice

1492 Christopher Columbus discovers the New World

1494–1559 France and Spain invade disunited Italy

1498 Savonarola burned at the stake

1503 Julius II, patron of the arts, becomes Pope

1504 Leonardo da Vinci paints the "Mona Lisa"

1504 Michelangelo completes his statue of "David"

1510 Pope Julius II and Venice form Holy League to drive French out of Italy

1510 Raphael at work in the Vatican, Rome

1527 Sack of Rome by Spaniards and Germans fighting for the Holy Roman emperor

1543 Vesalius publishes his work on human anatomy

1559 Treaty of Cateau-Cambrésis. Habsburg Spain established as dominant power in Italy

Independent states

At this time, Italy was not a single nation. Instead it was made up of many different states, some large and some tiny, each with its own government. Southern Italy formed the Kingdom of Naples. In central Italy lay the Papal territories. This was a large area of towns and countryside controlled from Rome by the pope, the head of the Roman Catholic Church. The chief states in the north included Florence, Genoa, Milan, and Venice.

During the Middle Ages the Holy Roman emperors (rulers from northern Europe) had controlled much of Italy. They had often been at war with the popes. By the end of the 13th century the Empire had been defeated by the Papacy. But the power of the Papacy itself was weakened by arguments over who should be pope. With the emperors and the popes weakened, the Italian cities were able to grow more powerful and rich.

The capital of an independent Italian state usually had strong walls to keep out invaders. In peacetime at least, it controlled the surrounding countryside. Compared with modern states and cities, these independent communities were very small. Padua, which had about 15,000 inhabitants in the late 13th century, was of average size. Florence at the same time had perhaps 100,000 inhabitants. It was then one of the largest cities in Europe. The usual distance between independent towns in northern Italy was only about 45 kilometers (25 miles).

These neighboring states were normally jealous of one another, and often went to war. When they were not fighting outsiders, members of a state were often fighting one another. Their

Goldsmiths in Florence. Trading brought great wealth to the city, and skilled craftsmen produced fine goods for its citizens to buy.

9

Lorenzo de' Medici, known as Lorenzo the Magnificent. He was given this title by his admirers, for he was a man of many ideas who encouraged learning, both in the arts and sciences. This bust was carved by the Florentine sculptor Verrocchio in the 15th century.

Below right: The lion of St Mark, the symbol of Venice, often appears in Venetian paintings and on buildings. Here it has been painted by the Venetian artist Carpaccio.

Below: The Arsenal at Venice, where its ships were built. Trade by sea with Muslim countries brought Venice immense wealth.

governments were not usually democratic, and the poor could not influence their rulers. Instead, a few rich families, or even a single family, often controlled a state for generations. Sometimes rich families fought each other. Sometimes the poor fought the rich.

Trading wealth

Most of the important developments of the Renaissance took place in northern and central Italy. They were made possible by the new wealth of the region, which was partly the result of adventurous seafaring. Early in the Renaissance the two ports of Genoa and Pisa competed for seaborne trade. In 1284, however, Genoa managed to destroy the Pisan navy in a great sea battle. Pisa became poor because it could not protect its trading ships. To this day there are famous buildings in Pisa, including the Leaning Tower, which show how rich and powerful it was until this defeat. Genoa was also very wealthy. By the late 13th century its trading ships were reaching England and Flanders in northern Europe, and the Black Sea in the east. It was a Genoese, Christopher Columbus, who many years later discovered America.

By the late 13th century Florence too was very wealthy. This city was to make a more important contribution to the Renaissance than any other. In the early Renaissance it helped to produce the three great writers Dante Alighieri, Petrarch, and Boccaccio. But perhaps the most famous period in Florence's history is from 1434 to 1494, when the Medici family controlled the city. The wealth of this family had come from their banking business. Part of it was now used to encourage some of the most admired artists of all time, among them Brunelleschi, Uccello, Botticelli, and Michelangelo. The Medici family encouraged scholars to collect and study the writings of Ancient Greece and Rome, and built magnificent palaces, villas, and church buildings. They were also statesmen, helping to arrange alliances between cities and so preventing outbreaks of war on many occasions.

Even in its great days, Florence had important rivals. At the end of the 14th century Milan's power greatly increased under its ruler Gian Galeazzo Visconti. He also arranged for the building of Milan's great cathedral and collected a large library. His city remained powerful and wealthy long after his death in 1402.

The island city

Perhaps the most strange and beautiful of the Italian cities was Venice. It was built on an island in a lagoon, and its main highways were not streets but canals. Venice at times chose to dominate the sea rather than fight for power on land in Italy. Venetian trading ships, like those of Genoa, reached far to the north and east of Europe by the 13th century. Fighting ships, built in Venice's great naval yard (known as the Arsenal), protected its trading vessels. Venice ruled an empire in the eastern Mediterranean, which included the Greek island of Crete. Even today there are great ruined fortresses and barracks there and on the Greek mainland, which bear Venice's sign – the lion of St Mark. These once guarded the Venetian empire. In Venice itself there are many beautiful Renaissance buildings, and it was the home of great artists including Titian and the Bellini family.

The power of the Church

The Roman Catholic Church extended its power over the men and women of every Italian state. Many people chose to become monks or nuns, living lives of prayer in buildings set apart from the ordinary world. Friars (churchmen dedicated to a life of poverty and preaching in public) were heard and obeyed by many. The pope, as head of the Church, controlled more than his own lands around Rome. Almost all Italians accepted his decisions. A pope could persuade men to take part in a *crusade*, which was a war against people said to be enemies of the Church. If the pope threatened to withdraw the blessings of the Church from an Italian city, many of its inhabitants would anxiously try to soften his anger. Some popes supported the new learning and art of the Renaissance. Other popes believed that these developments threatened Christianity, and strongly opposed them.

A painting of the Villa Poggio which was built for Lorenzo de' Medici. Wealthy men built country villas with carefully laid out gardens. Beautiful and elegant buildings like this gradually replaced the fortified palaces of earlier days.

Doge Leonardo Loredan. The Doge was the Venetian head of state. This portrait was painted by Giovanni Bellini in 1501.

11

The Condottieri

Generals with bands of soldiers
were hired to fight for the city states.

In the many wars of Renaissance Italy,
communities often preferred not to risk
using their own citizens as soldiers.
Instead they hired a general with an
army from outside to do their fighting
for them. These generals made an
agreement, or contract, to fight for their
employer for a fixed time. They came to
be called *condottieri*, which means
"contract men". Some were foreigners,
some were the sons of poor farmers, and
some were even rulers themselves whose
little states could not be supported
without their earnings.

Among the most successful and
famous condottieri of the 15th century
were Francesco Sforza and Federigo da
Montefeltro. Francesco through his

The early 15th-century
condottiere Gattamelata
(his name means
''honeyed-cat''). He carries
a commander's baton in
his right hand, and he is
wearing armor in the
style of Ancient Rome.
His horse is shown in a
lifelike way, with veins
standing out on its head
and belly. This bronze
statue was cast by
Donatello in the middle of
the 15th century.

Left: The 15th-century
condottiere Filippo
Scolari, painted in
magnificent armor by
Andrea del Castagno. The
armor does not completely
cover his elbows because
his arms had to bend
freely. Filippo Scolari was
born in Florence, but
served as a condottiere
under a ruler of Hungary.

successes became ruler of Milan.
Federigo used the profits from his own
campaigning to increase the beauty of the
city he ruled, Urbino (see page 14). But if
a condottiere disappointed his employer,
severe punishment might follow. The
general Carmagnola, after winning great
victories, failed to satisfy the government
of Venice, which employed him; so he
was tricked into coming back to Venice,
and there he was publicly beheaded.

Military tactics

The condottieri and their main troops
usually fought on horseback and in
armor. Such cavalrymen were often
defeated when their horses were
attacked; when the wounded horse
collapsed, its rider was brought crashing
to the ground. But the outstandingly
successful 14th-century condottiere Sir
John Hawkwood, an Englishman
employed by several Italian cities,
preferred to use footsoldiers rather than
cavalry. These were formed into small
groups, which bristled with lances and

The siege of a town from a painting of about 1370. In the center a soldier prays that God will help the attack. His prayer seems to be answered: a saint (with a halo) is shown knocking down the defenses of the town. The townspeople look out from behind their crumbling walls and towers.

were very difficult to attack. In addition, Hawkwood used archers with English longbows. These bows could pierce armor and pin a cavalryman to his own saddle. To impress and frighten his enemies, Hawkwood got his men to polish their breastplates until they were dazzling. Because of this they became known as "the White Company".

Comrades in arms

Condottieri in battle sometimes felt more sympathy for the condottieri on the other side than they did for their own employers. Employers might well be treacherous, while the rival condottieri shared the same way of life and might even, one day, fight on the same side. After defeating and capturing several famous condottieri and their armies, Carmagnola on one occasion simply let them all go free. During another battle opposing condottieri are said to have exchanged polite messages, promising not to shoot arrows at each other. But condottieri could behave very badly at

times. Even Carmagnola was not always generous. He once killed captives in front of their own relatives. Hawkwood also once organized a great massacre of unarmed townspeople. But casualties in battles were often few.

ARMOR
Condottieri and their soldiers were often saved by their armor. This protected the body well, and was difficult to pierce, except with arrows from a longbow. Sometimes a warrior suffered more from the heat inside his armor than from the enemy outside. During one long battle under a hot sun, "a terrible sighing" was said to have been heard from inside the helmets as the poor warriors became overheated. The great weight of armor could be dangerous, too. The father of Francesco Sforza, himself a famous condottiere, was drowned after falling off his horse into a river. His heavy armor prevented him from swimming to safety.

Rich and Poor

Wealthy citizens enjoyed luxuries and learning, but the poor lived in squalor and disease.

During the Renaissance rich people often lived elegant and even luxurious lives. But they were often far from idle. Wealthy merchants and bankers spent long hours at business and yet found time to study the authors of Ancient Greece and Rome, to go to and give elaborate feasts, and to help in the government of their cities. Lorenzo de' Medici, one of the great banking family who lived in Florence, wrote poetry and songs and was a good amateur architect; he was famous as a statesman and still had time to run several country estates and breed racehorses. At the courts of the ruling families, courtiers were expected to be learned and skilled in many ways. A 16th-century writer said that a courtier should know Latin and Greek, and should be a reasonably good musician and painter. His main skill should be as a soldier. To be truly graceful and cheerful at court he should also be in love!

Federigo da Montefeltro, the clever and kind ruler of Urbino in the 15th century. Much of his wealth came from his campaigns as a condottiere. In one fight he received an ugly wound on the right side of his face. To hide his scars he is shown from the left in this painting by Piero della Francesca.

Rich and elegant men and women wearing fine clothes attend a wedding in Florence in the early 15th century. This scene is from a painting on the front panel of a wooden chest or "cassone".

A generous ruler

One of the most cultured Italian cities was Urbino, especially during the reign of Duke Federigo da Montefeltro (1422–1482). He spent much of his money in building schools and hospitals for his people at Urbino, as well as in the

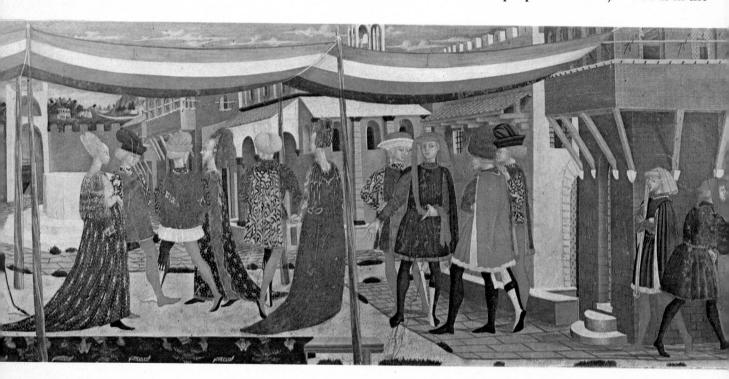

construction of churches, monasteries, and a palace containing his famous library (see page 29).

Federigo seems to have been very popular with his subjects. He was able to walk in public, and to talk to the ordinary people he met, without having a bodyguard of soldiers. It was said that no other ruler at that time dared to do this.

Federigo showed much concern for the poor in his city. Other men of the Renaissance spent their money more selfishly. In the early 16th century a banker called Agostino Chigi had fittings of solid silver made for his bathroom, and slept on a bed made of ivory and silver. At one famous feast which he gave in Rome he wished to show off his wealth to his guests. After every course of the meal he told his servants to throw the silver serving dishes into the river Tiber. His guests were meant to think that he could afford to lose them all. But beforehand he had laid nets in the river to catch the silver. When his guests had gone home, Chigi got his silver back!

Poverty

Luxury and elegance helped to make the Renaissance famous. But at the same time many Italians were desperately poor. Urbino was praised for having no beggars, but elsewhere things were very different. In 1457 there were some 30,000 pauper families in Florence – nearly a third of the population. At Venice begging became so serious a problem in the winter of 1528–1529 that the government banned it. Wages were very low for workers in the cloth industry, and workers at the Venice Arsenal were often paid late.

In the country the peasant's life could also be very hard. Large landowners, including the Church, rented out the land. Some leases were as short as three years. The peasant would work the land on a crop-sharing basis, supplying the owner with animals and produce. Relations between peasant and land-owner were often very bad, and there were many revolts. In parts of Italy there were still serfs well into the 15th century.

In this woodcut peasants are shearing sheep. For poor people life in the country was often hard.

Slaves were imported from the eastern Mediterranean by the Venetians. Some were kept for domestic work; others were sold abroad. Profits from the slave trade helped to pay for the luxuries of rich Venetians. In several ways like this we can see how elegance and poverty existed side by side. In Venice, the publisher Aldus Manutius went to great pains to produce fine books. But in order to do so he made harsh economies. A visitor said that Aldus's employees were fed with bread made from moldy flour, and water was mixed with their wine. His house was drafty, and so dirty that in summer the bedbugs and fleas kept people awake.

A Negro takes a passenger in a gondola along the Grand Canal in this detail from a painting by Carpaccio. The Venetians kept slaves for a number of duties.

SCHOOLS AND UNIVERSITIES

Federigo's schools at Urbino were not the only good ones in Italy. At many other schools corporal punishment was forbidden, and boys and girls were sometimes educated together. At the famous school run by Guarino da Verona in the 15th century, Latin and Greek literature were the main subjects. History and astronomy, mathematics and natural history were also taught, with games, swimming, and dancing. This school was mainly for the children of the rich, though a few poor boys were admitted free of charge. Universities helped to educate older students. During the 12th and 13th centuries many new universities were founded – to meet the need of businessmen and rulers for clever, well-educated helpers.

SQUALOR AND DISEASE

The streets of Italian cities usually stank. In Venice spices were burned in public to hide the unpleasant smells. Disease flourished in the dirt and poverty. Especially terrible was the Black Death, a plague carried by rats and fleas. It was brought to Italy in 1347 by a ship from the Crimea in southern Russia. It spread from Genoa, where the ship docked, all through Europe. The Black Death killed perhaps one-third of the population of Italy. Apart from causing this appalling number of deaths, the disease had several strange effects. At Florence the poor were said to be unwilling for a time to do any work. Why work to earn money if one would soon die anyway from the Black Death? It seemed better to enjoy the few days that might remain. As many laborers died, and others refused to work, employers had to pay high wages to attract workmen. It was often thought that the Black Death was a punishment from God. Many people went in processions, whipping themselves. They hoped that if they punished themselves like this, God would spare them from the punishment of the Black Death.

Pensions and charity

At Venice special arrangements were made to help some of the elderly workers. Until 1440 there was a rule that one in every six shipbuilding workers had to be over 55. It was meant to prevent workers simply being dismissed and left in poverty when they got old. This arrangement was eventually replaced by a pension scheme. Many people were not so lucky. Some who could not keep themselves would be helped by relatives or by Christian organizations. There were many religious charities, helping orphans, the old, and the sick. At Rome there was occasionally a strange compensation for the poor. When a cardinal was elected pope, the poor of the city were allowed to loot his former home, which would often be richly and generously furnished.

Local conflicts

Sometimes the people of a town divided into hostile groups. The rich (called "the sleek people") and the poor ("the little people") of a town might go to war with each other. Rich families tried to protect themselves by building their own private fortresses inside the town. These were tall towers, and many can still be seen today. In a crisis the rich could take refuge there, and defy the people below.

At other times the rich fought among themselves. A great victory in a civil war could mean that the losing side might be driven permanently out of the town. In this way the poet Dante was expelled from Florence in 1302, never to return. Often men in exile would spend years plotting ways in which they could return home or take revenge on their enemies. On a smaller scale, feuds were carried on for years between small groups and families. These were known as *vendettas*, and they could lead to horrible deeds, including murders.

On one occasion, a boy was accidentally killed by two others. His father took revenge. He killed one of the two, and cut out his liver. He then prepared the liver as part of a meal and fed it to the boy's own father. After the meal, he told the father that he had just eaten part of his own son. Many murders later followed between the families of the two fathers.

Ordinary thefts often involved murder. One Roman did not bother to report seeing the body of a murdered man being thrown into the Tiber river; he explained later that murder was so common that it hardly seemed worth reporting. In Venice the dark alleyways became so dangerous that the authorities banned the carrying of all sharp knives. In a country district a herdsman confessed to his priest that he had drunk a little milk during a religious fast. Later the priest found out that the herdsman often robbed and murdered travelers. He had not bothered to confess this, as robbery and murder did not seem so sinful as drinking a little milk at the wrong time!

Hunting was a favorite sport of the rich in Renaissance times. A group of does stands safely in the wood; noblemen hunted stags only.

COUNTRY PARTIES

Rich, well-educated men and women entertained one another at day-long parties in the countryside. The morning might start with a walk, and serious conversation about religion and philosophy. Then, during breakfast, music and singing would amuse the guests. Afterwards they would recite poems they had made up since the previous day. In the evening each guest would tell a story. At supper, the conversation would be lively but decent – so that the ladies would not be ashamed to listen. And the gentlemen were asked not to get very drunk.

Within easy reach of Florence there were many delightful villas where such parties could be held. One writer described them as standing "in clear air, amid cheerful scenery, and with a fine view: there is little fog and no harmful wind: all is good, and the water is pure and healthy".

Girls and Women

Well-educated women became writers, artists, and leaders in society.

In the Italian Renaissance people were eager to develop talent wherever it could be found. This meant that many people who could afford it arranged for girls to be educated as well as boys. A girl who attended school was often taught the same things as a boy. Some people objected to bringing up girls in this way. One man claimed that young ladies should not be allowed to play some ball games, ride, or wrestle. But male disapproval of this kind was often ignored.

Following their education, many women became famous in society. Several of the finest Italian poets were women. Vittoria Colonna, who was a granddaughter of Duke Federigo da Montefeltro, wrote impressive religious verse. She had learned some of the most recent Protestant theories from Germany (see page 39). Laura Battiferri, whose proud face is shown opposite, also wrote good religious poetry. The artist and poet

Wealthy and rather stout Venetian women, from a painting by Carpaccio. One is playing with two pet dogs. Both women seem to be staring in a bored way. Rich Italian women were discouraged from going out very often. Their lives must sometimes have been rather dull and restricted.

A harvest scene with women and men picking grapes for winemaking. Peasant women worked long hours in the fields. This detail is from an early 15th-century fresco: "Occupations of the Months".

Bronzino, who painted Laura's portrait, described her character as "a soul of steel in a body of ice".

At parties women were often more important than men, and directed the activities of the guests. Some women had sharp wits and a sharp tongue which men could easily be afraid of. The beautiful and kind Isabella de Luna was a popular member of high society, but she used shocking language to get her way.

Women at war

Women were also important in politics and warfare. Lucrezia Borgia was the daughter of the evil Roderigo Borgia, who became Pope Alexander VI. As pope he twice put Lucrezia in charge of the Vatican City at Rome, while he was away. He could clearly rely on her to be competent and tough. Bianca Maria Visconti, one of the family who ruled Milan in the 1400s, understood the people of her city and was popular with

them. Her advice and popularity were a great help to her husband, Francesco Sforza, when he came to rule Milan. Bianca was also a warrior. Once, when her husband was away, she led a successful attack on a hostile fortress. On another occasion she commanded troops in battle against an enemy force from Venice. She is said to have killed a Venetian soldier with a throw of her spear. And women often accompanied soldiers when they went to war although, if their army was defeated, they ran the risk of being shared out among the men of the winning side as "spoils of war"! A lady called Bona went on campaign (wearing male dress) with her lover, the condottiere Brunoro. When he was captured, she spent many years traveling great distances to visit powerful men, hoping that they might help her win his freedom. In the end she succeeded, and she and Brunoro were married.

Even so, women were often very strictly controlled by men. Marietta, the daughter of the prosperous Venetian artist Tintoretto, was brought up to be a good painter herself. Her reputation spread, and she was invited to go abroad, to work at royal courts. But her father refused to let her go. Marietta was not allowed to have an independent career.

Marrying into danger

Girls were expected to marry when they were still very young, often only 14. They were frequently made to marry someone chosen by their father. A rich

In this woodcut a country woman milks a cow, while her husband works beside her churning milk.

father was expected to give a large sum as dowry to his daughter's husband. Often a father would use this money selfishly, and choose a son-in-law who would provide him with valuable friendship, rather than his daughter with a good husband. If a wife was unfaithful to her husband, and loved another man, she could be severely punished. In Ferrara wives could even be burned at the stake.

Some men strongly disapproved of such harsh treatment of women. One man wrote that every day he heard dreadful stories of women being punished. "This man has murdered his wife because he suspected her of being unfaithful. Another man has killed his daughter because of a secret marriage. Someone else has had his sister murdered because she would not marry as he wished. It is very cruel of us men to claim the right to do whatever we please, while not allowing the poor women to do the same. If they do anything which does not please us, there we are at once with cords and daggers and poison." Even for women of rich families life could often be dangerous and distressing.

Laura Battiferri, the 16th-century poetess, painted by Bronzino. She wears somber but elegant clothes with a fine headdress and a delicate veil. Bronzino said Laura had a strong personality, as her firm nose and chin seem to suggest.

The port of Livorno (Leghorn) in northwest Italy was built partly by the Medici family of Florence to encourage trade. Here it is shown on a colored marble and stone table top made in the middle of the 16th century.

Wealth from overseas

Much of Italy's wealth was the result of trade. Goods like cloth, silk, and spices were quite plentiful, and so quite cheap, in some parts of the world. In other parts of the world they were much rarer, and so they were much more expensive. Italian traders bought these goods in countries where they were cheap. Then they transported them to other parts of the world, and sold them at far higher prices. Much of the profit gained in this way was then taken back to Italy. Many fine goods were sold for use in Italy itself. Probably the luxurious imported goods which were sold in the Italian towns encouraged wealthy people to become wealthier still – so that they could buy even more of these tempting things.

Italian merchants traveled to many distant countries in their search for goods. In northern Europe they bought wool and cloth from England, Flanders (modern Belgium), and northern France to sell elsewhere. Some of the cloth was taken to Italy, where it was dyed and reworked to make it finer. Then it was sold for much more money to people in Africa and the East. By the early 14th century Florence made more fine cloth than anywhere else in Italy. The glorious works of art in Florence were largely made possible by the profits from this cloth trade. Italian traders in the East

Trade and Exploration

Merchants grew wealthy through trade, and their search for new routes led to the discovery of the New World.

The wonderful ideas, the fine buildings, and the works of art of the Italian Renaissance probably would never have been produced unless many men and governments had been rich. Finding wages for artists and scholars was expensive. It cost a great deal to pay architects, craftsmen, and laborers, and to transport building materials. Even sending children to school cost a lot. School fees usually had to be paid, and parents lost the money the children could have earned if they had been sent to work instead. Italy was better able to meet these important expenses than other European countries were. Where did this great Italian wealth come from?

A 14th-century map of part of Asia. It shows Marco Polo on one of his long trading journeys. Camels carry his goods, while horses carry the traders themselves.

were interested in a far wider range of goods. Venice and Genoa sent groups of traders to live around the Black Sea and buy salted fish, leather, and furs from Russia to be sold elsewhere.

New markets
During the early Renaissance great Christian expeditions, called crusades, were organized in western Europe to protect Christian pilgrims who traveled to the Bible Lands and later set up Christian kingdoms there. Many Italians supported the conquering crusaders because they hoped to trade in the newly conquered areas. The Fourth Crusade in 1204 captured the Byzantine capital of Constantinople – although it was a Christian city. Venice did much to support this crusade, and profited greatly by it. Venetian traders got great privileges in the busy markets of Constantinople. Later, in 1261, Venice's rival Genoa made an alliance with the Greek emperor of Constantinople. He regained control of his city in that year, and Genoa was given the chief position in the city's trade.

Italians traveled far east for the sake of trade, sometimes to India, or even to China. To carry goods back to Europe from these distant countries was extremely expensive. Much had to be spent on food, clothes, and baggage animals during the long months of traveling. To make this expensive journey worthwhile, the merchants had to carry a very precious and profitable load indeed. This meant that merchants made an attractive target for thieves and pirates. Great courage was needed to travel on the Far Eastern routes.

Taxes and loans
The governments of Italian trading cities taxed the imported goods which were brought into their territories, gaining great wealth by doing so. In 1293 the harbor taxes of Genoa brought in seven times as much as the yearly income of the king of France. With an income like this, a small Italian state could become a great power in the Mediterranean world.

A trader in the Renaissance, like a trader today, often needed a loan to buy goods, before he could sell them and make his profit. Many banks came into existence to supply these loans, and to make a profit for themselves by charging interest on the loans. Some Italian bankers were well known throughout Europe. At the end of the 13th century King Philip IV of France had bankers from Florence as his advisers. King Edward III of England got badly into debt, and came to owe over a million and a quarter florins to a firm of bankers in Florence. In 1338, after he refused to pay, the wretched firm was ruined. Very often, however, bankers succeeded in bringing great wealth into Italy.

Journey to Cathay
The search for profits from trade led some men into distant explorations. In the 1370s Marco Polo, a trader from Venice, bravely traveled into the heart of

A Florentine gold florin of 1435. This is the actual size of the florin.

A banker dealing with a customer. The early Italian banks were stalls or benches set up in the market. The word bank comes from the Italian word "banca" which means bench.

Christopher Columbus, the Italian explorer who discovered America. He holds a navigational instrument. Life for sailors was often dangerous and dirty, and food on board ship went bad on long voyages.

Ambassadors from Venice talk with a Muslim ruler. Notice the domed mosque (a Muslim place of worship) on the left, and the Arabic writing above the gateway. This picture was painted by a Venetian artist in 1512.

Kublai Khan, ruled from Khan-balik (Peking). Marco Polo traveled over more of the world than anyone is known to have done before him. The lively tales of his travels, which he helped to write, are still good to read. After the Polos' explorations Italian trade with China became quite common for a time.

A new route to China?

Many years later, in the late 15th century, Marco Polo's tales were read with fascination by an Italian from Genoa called Christopher Columbus. He too decided to travel to China. But by Columbus's time the land route to China could not be used. Peoples along the route had become hostile to western travelers. So Columbus, with money and support from the court of Spain, tried to reach China not by traveling east, but by sailing west around the world. In trying to do this in 1492 he discovered a continent blocking his way. This was America. The American lands were not to be exploited by Italian states, but the discovery of America was one of the greatest achievements of the Italian Renaissance.

the great Mongol empire. This empire stretched over most of Asia in the 13th and 14th centuries, and because of its fierce warriors many Europeans thought of it as a terrifying place. The young Marco Polo, traveling with his father and uncle, reached Cathay (China), where the great emperor of the Mongols,

Art and Architecture

New interest in art brought beauty to Italian cities and houses, and fame to artists.

During the Middle Ages, painting, sculpture, and architecture were thought of as crafts. The powerful trade guilds who ordered works of art used standard pattern books for guidance, and gave strict instructions to the craftsmen they employed. These workers would never have dreamed of signing their work as their own.

During the Renaissance a change took place which was the most noticeable in Florence. There, wealthy bankers and traders built splendid houses which they decorated with beautiful portraits and sculptures. Lorenzo de' Medici began a school for artists where boys were taught a wide knowledge of the arts and sciences. He invited artists to dine with him, treating them as friends, not workmen. Artists were encouraged to read and study the works of the past, and to think of new techniques in art and building. Men like Michelangelo, Leonardo da Vinci, and Raphael were famous throughout Italy, and beyond. They were very different from the humble, anonymous craftsmen of the Middle Ages.

The wealthy men of Florence, like the Medici family, admired *classical* (Ancient Greek and Roman) styles and encouraged their artists to do the same. They hoped to recreate the wonders of Ancient Rome, which must have been an inspiration to them as well as a great sadness. For Rome itself was now crumbling away and overgrown with weeds. Cosimo de' Medici arranged for a traveler to send him descriptions of the Parthenon temple in Greece, of buildings in Asia Minor, and of the pyramids in Egypt. These descriptions strengthened the Florentines' belief that art should use

The "Betrothal of the Virgin" by Raphael, painted in oil in about 1504. People wear Renaissance clothes in this imaginary scene of Mary and Joseph becoming engaged. The circular church behind them has columns and rounded arches similar to those of Ancient Roman buildings. Raphael's use of perspective helps to show distance; the pavement lines get closer together as they near the church, and the people in the background are smaller than those in the front.

regular mathematical forms, above all the square and the circle. But Church authorities objected to the idea of circular churches!

Renaissance ideas in art started to spread after about 1400. Artists tried to find the best ways of showing people and objects realistically, and experimented with new kinds of paint. By 1500 many of them had mastered these techniques. Soon they started to look for different ways of presenting their subjects. They still often used classical themes but they showed people in twisted poses and with strangely proportioned bodies.

During the Renaissance many of the most admired and best known architects, sculptors, and artists produced some of the most famous works in history.

Architecture

Before the Renaissance the main style of medieval architecture, especially in northern Europe, had been Gothic. Buildings in this style are usually tall and narrow, with towers, spires, and pinnacles. Arches are delicately pointed and the dark mysterious interiors, with their tremendous heights, are often lit by narrow windows of stained glass.

The new churches and houses of the Renaissance were modeled largely on buildings of Ancient Rome. They had rounded arches and broad windows which made their interiors light. The picture below shows a chapel designed by Brunelleschi, who was the architect of some of the finest buildings in Florence. The decorations were also copied from classical buildings. Brunelleschi had traveled between Rome and Florence for about 12 years, examining classical architecture, studying mathematics, and making clocks in his spare time to earn some money. He spent hours crawling over the roofs of Roman buildings, and even removed the tiles to find out more about techniques the Romans used.

Brunelleschi used what he had learned about Roman building methods in his design for the great dome of Florence

The Pazzi Chapel in Florence, designed by Brunelleschi and built in about 1430. The proportions and decorations are similar to the buildings of Ancient Rome. The gray pilasters (columns) help to divide the space into regular forms and give the little chapel the character of a classical building.

cathedral. The builders had come to a halt, since no one knew how to build a dome on the vast scale that was needed. At first Brunelleschi's ideas seemed extraordinary, but he knew they had worked in Roman times and he persuaded the people of Florence that they would be suitable now. The height of the dome from the ground to the roof was 82 meters (270 feet) – the largest dome anyone had built (see page 8).

In the 13th and 14th centuries Italian houses had been built rather like fortresses, with towers at their corners and battlemented roofs. They were designed for strength, not beauty. The new houses in Florence were designed to be delightful places to live in. In 1490 Lorenzo de' Medici turned one of his country houses into a villa with ideas from a Greek temple (see page 11).

Gardens for the new villas were laid out according to classical styles. Flower beds and paths were arranged to form regular patterns which were often based on squares and circles. Flowering trees were planted regularly along the paths and formed covered ways leading to the houses. People also decorated their gardens with fountains and statues, following the classical style.

Sculpture

In 1402 a goldsmith called Ghiberti won a competition to design paneled bronze doors for the Baptistery building in Florence. His sample panel illustrated Abraham, a biblical prophet, sacrificing his son Isaac, who is shown naked (see page 5). Classical sculptors had often shown male nudes and Ghiberti was following their example. A medieval sculptor would have made sure that Isaac was dressed in flowing robes! For the next 21 years Ghiberti worked on the doors, making scenes from the life of Christ. Immediately he had finished them he was asked to make another pair of doors, which took him another 27 years. Many artists, including one of the most famous Renaissance sculptors, Donatello, began their training as apprentices in his vast workshop.

Part of the great cathedral of Milan, designed in the Gothic style in the late 14th century. Lines of pinnacles decorate its roof. Gothic buildings are often tall and have pointed arches and windows.

Michelangelo's famous marble statue of "David" which he finished in 1504 when he was only 29. Michelangelo has shown David naked in classical style, with curly hair and a straight nose.

The "Tribute Money" by Masaccio, painted in fresco in about 1428. The well-rounded figures stand firmly on the ground. Notice how the building on the right seems to go farther back into the pictures and how the hills appear to be in the distance. Masaccio was one of the first artists to use perspective correctly.

MAJOR. ARTISTS
(with page numbers of works illustrated)
Florence:
Giotto
(c. 1267–1337; p. 36)
Masaccio
(c. 1401–c. 1428; p. 25)
Uccello
(c. 1396–1475; p. 42)
Piero della Francesca
(c. 1415–1492; p. 14)
Botticelli
(c. 1445–1510; p. 27)
Leonardo da Vinci
(1452–1519; pp. 26, 35, 43)
Raphael
(1483–1520; p. 23)
Michelangelo
(1475–1564; pp. 24, 26, 38)
Bronzino
(1503–1572; p. 19)
Venice:
Mantegna
(c. 1431–1506; p. 7)
Giovanni Bellini
(c. 1430–1516; pp. 11, 27)
Carpaccio
(c. 1460–c. 1523; pp. 10, 15, 18)
Titian
(c. 1487–1576; p. 37)

In 1443 the city of Padua paid Donatello to make a bronze monument to the condottiere Gattamelata, showing him on horseback. Bronze casting on so large a scale had not been tried since Roman times. Donatello had spent a long time studying Roman ruins and sculptures with Brunelleschi, and the monument he produced looks like that of a Roman general. He even showed Gattamelata wearing classical armor (see page 12). Many other sculptors followed his ideas, and produced large figures.

In 1505 Pope Julius II instructed Michelangelo to make him a huge tomb with 40 large figures, but they soon quarrelled and when he eventually finished the tomb nearly 40 years later it was very much smaller.

Painting

Before the Renaissance, painting in Italy was mostly influenced by the Byzantine style from the eastern Mediterranean. Religion was the chief theme. Often tall, stern-faced saints and angels were shown against flat gold backgrounds (see page 42). There was little feeling of distance between the figures, and it did not seem to matter if they were all the wrong size in relation to one another.

Around 1300 a painter called Giotto broke away from this style. He tried to paint people more realistically, and with human expressions. He tried to make his figures look solid and to set them against real-looking backgrounds (see page 36).

At the beginning of the 15th century artists began to combine Giotto's ideas with those of classical times. The Ancient Romans thought that *proportion* was very important, and Renaissance artists began to work out rules for their paintings. Objects and figures were based on the most perfect proportions. The head, for instance, was one-seventh the length of the body.

Artists were particularly interested in the problem of *perspective*, which meant making the objects in the background of a picture seem the right size and shape compared with the objects in the foreground. Brunelleschi noticed that the parallel lines of green and white marble on the walls of the Baptistery in Florence seemed to get closer together the farther from him they were. Using his observations artists worked out rules for showing perspective in their pictures.

Masaccio was one of the first artists to follow Brunelleschi's theories, and the picture above shows his use of perspective. He also managed to make his

FRESCO
Fresco painting was used to decorate walls and ceilings. Layers of plaster were spread over the walls, and then powdered colors mixed with water were quickly painted onto the final layer of plaster while it was still wet. Sections of wall to be painted were freshly plastered each day so that the surface was always damp. Mistakes in fresco were difficult to correct once the plaster had dried. To avoid such mistakes, artists first made sketches on paper of the paintings they planned. These sketches were called *cartoons*. When a cartoon was finished, holes were pierced along the outlines of the design and the cartoon was fixed to the section of wall to be painted that day. Charcoal dust was sprinkled over it which went through the pierced holes. The cartoon was then removed from the wall, and the artist could see the marks of the dust on the plaster, showing the design he now had to follow.

EGG AND OIL

Until the late 15th century *tempera* was the most popular technique for all paintings except those on walls. Finely powdered colors were mixed to a sticky paste with egg. The mixture was painted onto a wooden panel which had been covered with several coats of very fine plaster. Tempera dried quickly and formed a very hard surface.

Sometime in the middle of the 15th century oil painting was introduced into Italy from northern Europe. It took a long time for Italian artists to become expert in its use, and many pictures were ruined while they were learning. Powdered colors were usually mixed with linseed oil and applied in several layers onto a wooden panel or a piece of stretched canvas. Since oil dries much more slowly than tempera, many artists welcomed this new form of paint. They were able to spend far more time working on their pictures, and even correcting mistakes, before the paint dried.

Grinding down different colored earths for paints and preparing surfaces was the job of young apprentices in an artist's workshop. While they were learning they would paint the easier sections, and then the master would come along and paint the more difficult parts!

figures look very solid, by noticing how light fell on objects and carefully painting in the shadows. Masaccio died in 1428 when he was only 27 but his ideas were used by other artists in Florence. Among them was Uccello. He was very interested in perspective (see page 42) and often chose to draw his subjects from strange angles.

Masaccio's paintings are mostly of religious subjects, but the painters who followed him often illustrated classical stories or painted portraits of rich people.

The "Mona Lisa", painted in oil in about 1504 by Leonardo da Vinci, is perhaps the best-known painting in the world. The shadows on the woman's cheeks, forehead, and hands give her a wonderfully rounded and delicate appearance. Portrait painters of the Renaissance liked to show landscapes in the distance. Here there is a romantic scene of a road winding between cliffs.

Religious subjects remained common, although sometimes when an artist like Raphael painted a portrait of the Virgin Mary, it was really a portrait of his own mistress! The painting of beautiful women, whether for a religious purpose or not, was a favorite activity of Renaissance artists. The portrait above is by Leonardo da Vinci and it is probably the most famous of all paintings.

Leonardo finished very few paintings since he was often kept busy by his work as an engineer and inventor (see page 35). Some of his paintings have not lasted well because he experimented with different kinds of paint. He used tempera instead of fresco for a vast wall painting of the Last Supper, and even in his own lifetime the paint was flaking off the wall.

Another Renaissance artist skilled at a number of activities was Michelangelo. As well as being a great sculptor he was a good architect, a poet, and one of the finest painters who ever lived. His most famous work as a painter is the series of religious scenes on the huge ceiling of the Sistine Chapel in Rome. This work was begun in 1508, and shows episodes from the Book of Genesis in the Bible, including the Creation of Man. The area

The Holy Family by Michelangelo, painted in tempera in 1504. Many 16th-century artists painted people in twisting positions like this. In the background are naked men looking very much like classical statues.

"Primavera" (Spring), painted by Botticelli in about 1478. Many of his paintings show beautiful women in scenes from classical stories. Here Cupid is shooting an arrow at one of the three dancing Graces to make her fall in love with the god Mercury, on the left of the picture. Venus, goddess of love, stands in the center, and to the right Flora (as the Spring) scatters roses on the grass.

which Michelangelo had to decorate was over 900 square meters (10,000 square feet). The fresco technique, which was needed for the painting, was something in which he had little practice.

Doing this work, all alone on his scaffolding under the great ceiling, was very uncomfortable for Michelangelo. He worked standing up, and had to strain back his head to paint the plaster above him. His watercolor paints sometimes dripped into his eyes. He also worried that he might never be paid for his work, but eventually his employer gave him what he had promised.

Painting in Venice

In Florence artists had worked out firm mathematical rules. In Venice painters became famous for the vivid colors they used in their work. Perhaps this was because Venice traded a great deal with the East. The silks, furs, jewelry, and oriental carpets they imported all made the Venetians notice color and textures. They made good use of the new technique of painting in oils in the second half of the 15th century. With it they produced wonderfully rich and glowing colors, and painted velvets,

silks, and furs so skillfully that you can almost feel their softness.

Florence and Venice were two of the most important centers of painting in Italy. But artists were at work in many cities painting portraits and decorating houses and religious buildings in the new style. Their ideas spread rapidly and helped the development of painting in most European countries.

"A Young Woman at her Toilet", by the Venetian artist Giovanni Bellini, who also painted the Doge Leonardo Loredan on page 11. Venetian artists liked painting the colors and textures of beautiful materials. This young woman is sitting on a fine red oriental carpet.

The poet Dante Alighieri, who lived from 1265 to 1321, stands near the buildings of his native city Florence. In the background are scenes from his most famous poem, "The Divine Comedy". The poem tells of an imaginary journey through Paradise, Purgatory, and Hell. His guide through Paradise is his former lover, Beatrice. On the left in this picture, sinners are being led into Hell. The picture was painted in 1465.

Books and Libraries

Books were prized possessions in the Renaissance, and wealthy men built up great libraries.

Clever men and women during the Renaissance wanted to read the best books which could be found. But often books by great authors of the past were very hard to find. Sometimes only a few copies of an important book were known to exist in the whole of Europe. Many books were only to be found in the library of a monastery, where no one except the monks could read them.

Another difficulty was that very many of the most respected books were not written in Italian. They were in Latin (the language of Ancient Rome), or in Ancient Greek which only a few people could understand. The poet Petrarch had been proud to own a manuscript of Ancient Greek poetry by Homer, but he was not able to read it!

Searching for manuscripts
Several men made great efforts to make books easier to find and to understand. Pope Nicholas V in the mid-15th century, and later the publisher Aldus

Two pages from "The Dream of Poliphilus" published by Aldus Manutius in 1499.

Manutius, arranged for agents and spies to hunt for the manuscripts of important works, not only in Italy but in countries as far away as England and Poland. When found, these works were copied either by hand ("manuscript" means something written by hand) or later by printing. In this way many more people could read them.

Translators were paid quite large sums of money to put into Italian works which were written in Latin or Greek. Several of the people translating Ancient Greek were men who had fled to Italy after the great Greek-speaking city of Constantinople was captured by Turks in 1453.

Copying out a book by hand took a long time, so such copies were very expensive. Even so, some people built up great libraries. The famous library in Urbino was organized in the mid-15th century by the ruler of the town, Federigo da Montefeltro. He employed 30 or more skilled people to copy out manuscripts; his books were bound in crimson covers ornamented with silver. In Rome, Pope Sixtus IV built the first library to be heated in winter. Anyone could use it, for a small fee.

In the 1450s printing from metal type was invented in Germany. It soon spread down through Italy. Printed books could be produced more quickly and cheaply than handwritten copies. Now many people who were neither rich men nor churchmen were able to learn from books. This helps to explain the success of Renaissance Italy. In other parts of Europe, however, people from poor families were not encouraged to develop their talents as often as in Italy.

Writers in Italian

Three of the greatest Italian writers lived in the Renaissance, and all of them were connected with Florence. In the late 13th century Dante Alighieri wrote poems in his native language, a form of north Italian speech called Tuscan. Until Dante did this, Italians had often been ashamed to write in their own language. Instead they had preferred to write in French or in Latin. By writing beautiful poetry in Italian, Dante made other people feel that it could be a dignified language.

The other two writers followed Dante in using Italian. Petrarch, in the 14th century, wrote love poems to a lady he called Laura. Most of them were 14-line sonnets, a form of poem which some writers still use today. His friend Boccaccio was the first great writer of Italian prose. In his work *The Decameron* he describes incidents from ordinary life.

MAKER OF BEAUTIFUL BOOKS

The most famous publisher of the Italian Renaissance was called Aldus Manutius; he worked in Venice from 1490. He was especially interested in printing the works of the great writers of Ancient Greece and Rome. He used *italic* (sloping) letters which are said to be modeled on the writing of the poet Petrarch. They were beautifully clear to read: Aldus boasted that his print was almost as delicate as fine handwriting. His type for Greek letters was made by goldsmiths, who were highly skilled in intricate metalwork.

Aldus despised people who owned fine books but who kept them in private libraries, where hardly anyone could read them. He called these people "book-buriers". He was proud that the beautifully printed books that he published allowed many thousands of people to read the important writings of others.

The first italic type was made by Aldus Manutius in 1500.

St. Jerome in his study. St. Jerome died in 420, but he is shown here sitting at a desk similar to those used by Renaissance scholars. This picture was painted by the 15th-century artist Antonello da Messina who is believed to have introduced oil painting into Italy.

Luxury and Repentance

Stern preachers condemned the luxuries and vanities of the rich.

In the prosperity of the Renaissance some Italians lived in striking luxury. Many people were impressed by the beautiful houses of the rich, where they ate off silver dishes at extravagant feasts, and slept on soft beds in fine linen. Many of the rich were vain, and spent much money on fine clothes, while women bleached their hair blonde and added false hair pieces. Perfume was used lavishly: even money was sometimes perfumed to make payment more elegant. Some of the perfume used was very powerful. Its smell could still be detected on Renaissance objects until quite recent times.

However, there were some stern Christians, especially the traveling preachers called friars, who disapproved of such luxuries and vanities. They wished people to live in simplicity and poverty, as Christ was believed to have done. They thought that Christians who lived in great poverty, denying themselves comforts and sometimes even food, were more likely to see visions of God. Others, by living humbly, might come to think of God and Heaven as

making a wonderful contrast to their own poor existence on Earth. These Christians thought that luxuries made people proud of themselves, instead of humble. Many friars believed that they also made men and women more contented with this life, and less interested in thoughts of God and a better life after death.

Friars also objected, at times, to the literature and art of the Renaissance. They thought that too much respect was being shown to writers who were not Christians, like the Ancient Greek thinkers Plato and Aristotle. They were afraid that pagan thought and behavior would come back. Artists, by painting flattering portraits with beautiful landscapes, seemed to be encouraging people to be proud of themselves and to think of the beauties of this world, rather than of Heaven.

Sermons and prophecies

In the 15th century many Italian friars urged men and women to repent, and to give up their pride and luxury. They persuaded several groups of men to stop the deadly vendettas in which they were proudly taking part, and sometimes caused people to give up their luxuries.

The most powerful of these friars was Girolamo Savonarola. He thought that the new classical learning had made Florence a sinful city, and said so in sermons which many people listened to. Again and again he preached against their way of life, and told people to give up luxury and pleasure and return to a

Savonarola, the preacher who ruled Florence for a few years.

simple and hard-working life. He prophesied that Italy would be invaded, and that the Medici rulers of Florence would be driven out. When both events came true, people were deeply impressed. Many thought that God had given Savonarola the gift of prophecy.

Savonarola was made ruler of Florence – a position which he held from 1494 to 1498. As ruler, he announced that the true king of Florence was now Jesus Christ. Christ himself, in the New Testament, tells a follower to sell his possessions and to give the money to the poor. Savonarola had a rather different idea. He believed that luxurious possessions should be burned. He therefore had great bonfires built in the Piazza della Signoria in Florence. To these bonfires many people willingly brought their own precious possessions. These included fine books and paintings. Some of these fine things might have survived until today if it had not been for the bonfires.

Other luxurious possessions were burned against the wishes of their owners. Savonarola's government organized gangs of boys to invade rich people's houses and drag away precious things to the bonfires. Probably the boys found this fun. But sometimes the owners of the houses treated the boys roughly. In the end, the boys needed a special guard of adults, to protect them.

At one bonfire, so many precious things were piled up ready to be burned that a rich man from Venice offered to pay Florence 22,000 gold florins if he could have them all. But Savonarola's government would not allow this. Instead orders were given to paint the man's portrait. It was then put on the bonfire, and burned along with everything else as an insult.

Eventually Savonarola made many powerful enemies. These included the Pope, Alexander VI. Savonarola was sentenced to death, and he himself was burned on a bonfire in the same Piazza della Signoria, in May 1498. But for years afterwards there were many people in Florence who honored the memory of the friar who once made them repent.

Boys, dressed as angels, watch as precious objects and possessions are burned in the Piazza della Signoria. They had raided people's homes in search of fine things to place on the bonfire.

Fra Luca di Pacioli, a mathematician-friar who wrote a book on arithmetic and geometry. In this early 16th-century portrait he is demonstrating a theorem on a slate.

Studying the body

By the 16th century Italy led Europe in medical knowledge. Many doctors in Europe still trusted the writings of the Ancient Greek doctor Galen. But Vesalius, a scientist from Flanders who had come south to work at Padua, found that he could not trust Galen. He decided to explore the workings of the human body for himself. This he did by *anatomy* – cutting up and examining human corpses. By doing this he found that Galen had been wrong in several ways – for example, in his description of the heart. Vesalius had trouble in getting the dead bodies for his important work, because many people disliked his "interfering" with the dead. Vesalius had to steal bodies from graveyards, and sometimes needed to hide corpses in his own bed!

Science and Medicine

Scientists in the Renaissance made great advances in knowledge, but often angered Church authorities.

It often took courage to be a good scientist in the Renaissance. For many centuries men had accepted ideas about science put forward by the Ancient Greeks. We realize now that the Greeks' ideas were often very intelligent, but that they were often wrong. In the Renaissance, when these ideas were still widely believed, a scientist had to be brave to think that he alone knew better. Many people did not want to have the old ideas disproved. They were afraid that the ancient traditions of Christianity itself might be questioned. So scientists were sometimes threatened with stern punishment for having these new ideas. However, this did not stop many brilliant scientific ideas and inventions being produced at this time.

The 16th-century physician Vesalius made important discoveries about the human body. This drawing, from one of his books, shows the positions of different muscles. Vesalius's muscular man is drawn against a landscape with ruins in the classical style.

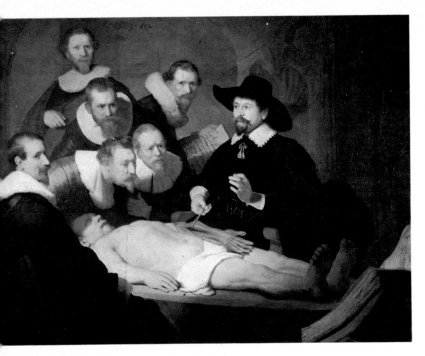

Another great doctor who worked at Padua was Realdo Colombo. In the 1550s he discovered that blood circulates between the heart and the lungs. His discovery was followed up by an Englishman, William Harvey, who had come to Padua to study at the end of the 16th century. Did the heart pump out nothing but new blood? Harvey showed that this was impossible. He measured the area inside the heart, and showed how much blood it could pump out. He then showed that if the heart was pumping out *new* blood all the time, in just a few hours it would pump out huge amounts of new blood weighing far more than the whole body! How could the heart be getting enough food or other material to turn into so much new blood? Harvey realized that the heart was not making so much new blood. Instead the blood was *circulating*. It was being pumped out from the heart, around the body, and back to the heart. Then it was pumped out again. William Harvey's Italian education had helped him to make one of the most important of all medical discoveries.

Causes for illness

Some Italian doctors became famous in faraway parts of Europe. In 1552 Girolamo Cardano was paid to make the

"The Anatomy Lesson of Dr Tulp", painted in 1632 by the famous Dutch artist Rembrandt van Rijn. By the 17th century the study of anatomy had at last become an accepted practice.

A marble bust of the physician Giovanni Chellini, one of whose patients was the sculptor Donatello. It was sculpted by Antonio Rossellino in 1456.

long journey from Italy to Scotland, to try to cure a Scottish archbishop of asthma. Cardano noticed that the asthma attacks seemed to happen when the archbishop was in bed. So he ordered that a different kind of bedclothes be used. The asthma was cured, and Cardano was given a huge reward. His explanation of the asthma attacks was roughly correct, though very unusual at the time. He believed that the complaint was caused by tiny, invisible particles entering the archbishop's lungs from his bedclothes.

Earlier, another Italian scientist called Girolamo Fracastoro had a similar important idea. He believed that some diseases were caused by minute, invisible organisms which could breed. These he called *seminaria*, which means "seed material". This idea, quite new in the 16th century, was close to the truth: Fracastoro's belief is similar to modern ideas about germs. But as the microscope had not yet been invented, Fracastoro was never able to see the tiny organisms which he rightly thought were there.

Scientist and artist

Another Italian scientist, Leonardo da Vinci, was one of the most brilliant men who has ever lived. He worked in the years around 1500, both as an artist and

FOSSILS

Fracastoro had an intelligent theory about fossils. He thought that these had been living creatures in ancient times. How, then, did fossils of sea-creatures come to be found on land? Fracastoro explained this, quite rightly, by saying that in an earlier age there had been water where in his time there was land. An Ancient Greek, Xenophanes, had explained fossils in a similar way over 2000 years before. But probably Fracastoro did not know this. Other Italians thought that fossils were "accidents"; although a fossil might *look* like a fish, they said, it had never been a fish. It had just been formed by chance in the same shape.

"The Ambassadors", painted in 1533 by the German artist Hans Holbein. Renaissance men were well educated in a number of subjects. These two men stand beside objects representing science, travel, music and literature. The strange object in the foreground is a skull. It is an optical illusion which "straightens out" when viewed close to from the right. The artist was demonstrating how well he could master his art, as well as reminding us of death.

Two of the telescopes used by the astronomer and physicist Galileo Galilei who lived from 1564 to 1642. He believed that the Earth moved around the Sun, and was one of the very first astronomers in Europe to use a telescope. He won the support of the government of Venice by showing how useful the telescope could be for observing enemy ships in wartime.

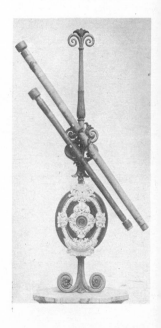

as a scientist. At this time art and science were not thought of as two subjects (as we think of them today) but as one. Both depended on accurate observation and close measurement of the world.

Leonardo had the imagination of a great artist, and a scientist's knowledge of how things worked. He became a brilliant inventor. He designed a war-machine on wheels, which was protected by armor like a tank. He drew sketches of machines with which he believed men could fly. He invented the idea of a parachute, and of explosive shells fired by cannon. It was centuries before other scientists had these ideas and put them into practice. After Leonardo's death many of his new ideas remained in his notebooks, unpublished and unknown. But one invention which Leonardo did put to work was a new design for a lock gate, to control the flow of water in rivers and canals. This design is still in use.

Barred by the Church

In the late Renaissance, about a century after Leonardo, Galileo Galilei, another clever Italian scientist, invented the thermometer and also built one of the first telescopes in the world. Most people in his day believed that the Sun went around the Earth. Galileo believed the opposite. With a telescope he saw the natural satellites of the planet Jupiter traveling in orbit around it. This made him more certain that the Earth was also in orbit – around the Sun. But Galileo's idea was felt to be an attack on the Christian view of the universe. He was ordered by the Church to give up his theory. He was threatened with torture if he did not say that the Sun moved around the Earth. Galileo was by then an old man, and he gave in, at least in public. The age of scientific discovery in Italy, and of the Italian Renaissance, was drawing to an end.

THE GREAT HORSE

Leonardo was a fine horseman, and one of his dreams was to cast the figure of a rearing horse in bronze, like his sketch shown on the left. In 1483, while Leonardo was in Milan, Lodovico Sforza asked him to make a statue of his father on horseback. Leonardo planned a bronze statue of a rearing horse, twice lifesize, with both front legs off the ground. About 90 tons of bronze were needed. Many people believed it would not be possible to cast such a statue, and so Leonardo changed to a pacing horse.

By 1493 Leonardo had finished a magnificent full-size clay model of the new horse, without its rider. It was this horse that brought Leonardo fame, even though he had already painted some of his finest pictures. Preparations were made for casting it. Sadly, this horse was never made either. The bronze that Lodovico Sforza had been collecting was used to make cannon. The model of the horse remained in Milan for only a few years longer. In 1499 French soldiers used it for target practice and it was ruined.

Below: This self-portrait shows Leonardo da Vinci, scientist, artist and inventor, in old age.

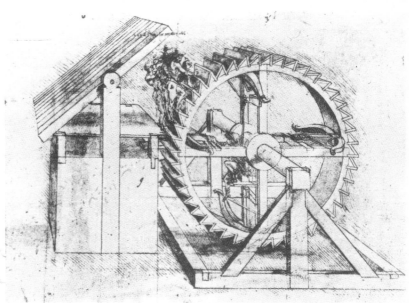

Above: Leonardo's design for a treadmill crossbow.

Below: Leonardo da Vinci has drawn a series of criss-crossing lines to help him show perspective.

The Church and Rome

St. Francis preaching to the birds, in a fresco painting thought to be by Giotto. St. Francis, who lived from 1182 to 1226, was a much loved traveling friar and preacher who founded the Franciscan order of friars. He and his followers lived in poverty and toward the end of his life he became a hermit. He was always very kind to animals and birds. In this picture the birds fly up to him with no fear.

Some Catholics respected the pagan worlds of Ancient Greece and Rome. Other Catholics found this horrifying. On one occasion Christ was said to be like the pagan god Apollo, and many people thought this a terrible insult. One pope described himself as "partly a god". This was the sort of boastful language which Ancient Roman emperors had used. But many thought Christians should be more humble. A more respected title for a pope was "servant of the servants of God".

The power and wealth of the Church were immense: Many popes and churchmen were holy and learned, while others were selfish and greedy.

One of the greatest powers in Renaissance times was the Catholic Church, which was the Church of Rome. In those days religion was very important in everyday life. Almost everyone believed in teachings of the Church. Traveling friars and parish priests preached to the people. Schools, hospitals, orphanages, and almshouses were run by priests and monks to look after the needs of the ordinary people.

In particular, people thought that if they lived sinful lives they would go to Hell. As they could only get forgiveness for their sins through the Church, they were particularly anxious to obey its rules. Sometimes rulers who made the Church authorities very angry were *excommunicated*, and this ban also applied to the people they ruled. It meant that they could not be baptized, married, forgiven their sins, or buried in a Christian way. It was an appalling punishment and the threat of excommunication gave the Church great power.

The pope, as head of the Church, was also a powerful ruler. His lands included Rome itself and a large area of central Italy. He and his officials were very rich. They ruled their subjects like ordinary rulers and often employed soldiers to fight for their interests.

People all over Europe carefully watched the way in which popes, cardinals, monks, and ordinary priests behaved. If these churchmen behaved well, many would imitate them. But if their behavior was bad, that too would be copied.

In many ways the Church during the Renaissance was very different from the Church today. Although high officials of the Church often acted in a wise and generous way, at other times their misbehavior was easy to see.

Patrons of art and learning

Several popes encouraged artists and scholars. Pope Nicholas, in the mid-15th century, paid the scholar Valla 500 ducats to translate the work of the historian Thucydides from Ancient Greek. Valla's earlier work had done much damage to the position of the pope. But Nicholas was still willing to recognize that Valla was a good scholar. Nicholas also paid for the collection of books to make a great library.

Another pope, Sixtus IV, built a library at Rome which anyone could use for a small charge. In ways like this several popes encouraged Italians to teach themselves, by learning from the cleverest thinkers of the past.

But in the late Renaissance the Church became frightened of the new learning. Several adventurous thinkers, among them the

A bronze medallion showing Julius II. He was a fierce and determined warrior, but also admired art.

Pope Paul III with his ''nephews'' (in fact, his sons) painted by the Venetian artist Titian. The young ''nephew'' on the right, wearing a sword, bows to the seated Pope who turns kindly towards him.

MAJOR RENAISSANCE POPES

Nicholas V (1447–1455)
A great supporter of the arts and literature

Pius II (1458–1464)
A patron of learning, and author of history and geography books and of poems in Latin

Sixtus IV (1471–1484)
Plotted against the Medici family; had Sistine Chapel built

Alexander VI (1492–1503)
Member of Spanish Borgia family; had several children; elected as pope through bribery; ordered execution of Savonarola; great supporter of the arts

Julius II (1503–1513)
Tried to extend papal lands; patron of Michelangelo and Raphael

Leo X (1513–1521)
Son of Lorenzo de' Medici; scholar and patron of arts; excommunicated Martin Luther

Clement VII (1478–1534)
Cousin of Leo X; taken prisoner when Rome was sacked

Paul III (1534–1549)
Called Council of Trent to reform the Church

brilliant scientist Galileo, were harshly treated for stating ideas the Church did not approve of.

Fine buildings for Rome

Several popes helped to give Rome fine buildings. Much of the city had become derelict. In the early 15th century weeds were growing in the streets, and wolves roamed around the center of the city. But Renaissance scholars read much about Ancient Rome. They learned of the glorious buildings the city had had during the Roman Empire, more than a thousand years earlier. Many people wished to bring back this glory. Perhaps the greatest of the new buildings which made people once more proud of Rome was the basilica of St. Peter's. This is still the most important church in the world for Roman Catholics. Its present building was begun by order of Pope Julius II in 1506. Julius also arranged for Michelangelo to paint the vast ceiling of the Sistine Chapel, which had been built in the reign of Sixtus IV. The result was one of the

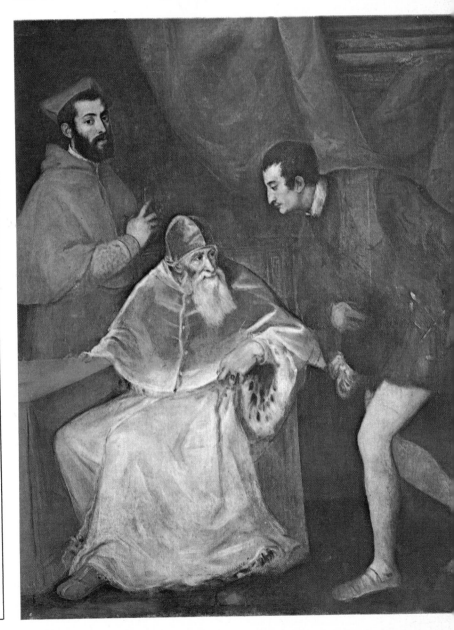

most famous works of art in the world. Raphael was another great Renaissance artist who worked for Julius in Rome. Some of his finest paintings decorate buildings there.

But Julius II had other interests besides architecture and art. He was a warrior, leading armies against his enemies. Popes in the Renaissance often acted more like ordinary rulers than as religious leaders. Pope Leo X loved hunting and once spent 37 days together on this sport. One of his senior officials complained that humble Christians were unable to kiss His Holiness's feet, because they were always covered in hunting boots! More seriously, several popes had mistresses and children, in spite of their sacred vows of *chastity*. Relatives of a pope were sometimes given special favors. Pope Innocent VIII, for example, appointed a relative of his own as cardinal – one of the highest officials of the Church. But the new cardinal was a boy of only 14.

Buying posts

High positions in the Church, like that of cardinal, were often given to men who would pay very highly for them – instead of to the men who were best fitted for the job. At one time bankers were put in charge of senior appointments. They seemed to be the best people to judge who had the most money to give! One cardinal claimed to have paid 60,000 ducats for his position. Another cardinal won the same huge sum in one night's gambling. Several senior churchmen were involved in murders, and the first handbook on the use of poisons was written by a cardinal from Florence. The Borgia family, two of whom became popes, have been remembered as poisoners ever after.

The behavior of the pope and his cardinals was imitated by many other churchmen. In the early 16th century Christians elsewhere in Europe became very angry at the corrupt ways and greed of some powerful Italian churchmen.

A bronze medallion showing Rodrigo Borgia. He was elected Pope through bribery in 1492, and took the name Alexander VI. He worked hard to increase his own power. He believed in killing his opponents, and ordered the execution of Savonarola. He had many lovers and several children. This medallion and the one on page 37 were made by the 16th-century medalist Paladino.

St. Peter's, Rome, seen from the Vatican Gardens. The buildings shown here were designed by Michelangelo, and include the famous dome which he helped to design. It was built in the 16th century.

The Legacy

In the 16th century Italy became less rich and important. But the ideas of the Italian Renaissance spread northward through Europe.

The effects of the Italian Renaissance were felt over most of Europe and its ideas were taken up by people outside Italy. By the 16th century, however, many people in Italy and in other European countries were opposed to the Renaissance. In 1510 a German Catholic, called Martin Luther, came to Rome. There he was annoyed by the careless way in which he thought that some priests were holding religious services. He also felt that it was wrong for non-Christian writers, like the Ancient Greek Aristotle, to be highly respected in Italy. Luther also disapproved of the Church authorities because they granted forgiveness of sins to people in exchange for money.

When he got back to Germany, Luther bitterly criticized the pope. The pope in turn criticized him. In 1520 Luther ceased to be a member of the Catholic Church, and set up his own organization of Christians in Germany. These became known as "Protestants": people who protested against certain beliefs and practices of the Catholic Church. The change from Catholicism to Protestantism in northern Europe is called the Reformation.

Studying the Bible

Luther and his Protestant followers believed that the words of the Bible should be studied very carefully – more carefully than Catholic thinkers often seemed to study them. Catholics had a deep respect not only for the Bible, but also for the decisions of the pope and for the traditional practices and teachings of the Church. But for Protestants what mattered most were the words of the Bible, which every Christian had a right to interpret for himself. Luther's followers distributed the Bible in a German translation, so that ordinary Christians in Germany could read it or hear it for themselves. In Catholic countries the Bible was only to be read in Latin. Since most ordinary people could not read Latin, all that they knew about the Bible was what the priests told them.

Before Luther's time, almost all Christians in western Europe had been Catholics. But now there were millions who were not. The movement spread. Many small northern European states turned to Protestantism. In England King Henry VIII quarrelled with the pope (who would not agree to Henry's divorce) and announced that he himself, and not the pope, was now head of the Church in England.

From the 16th century onward, there was much violent quarreling in Europe between Protestants and Catholics. In France the Protestants, known as Huguenots, were cruelly persecuted. In England in the 1550s the Roman Catholic Queen Mary had hundreds of English Protestants burned at the stake. After Mary's death, the Protestant Queen Elizabeth I made it illegal to worship in England as a Roman Catholic. Large fines were imposed upon anyone

In 1521 Martin Luther was excommunicated (deprived of Church membership) by Pope Leo X for criticizing the Roman Catholic Church. In this picture he is publicly burning the papal bull (document) ordering his excommunication. Luther and his followers, known as Protestants, gained much support. The movement he founded is known as the Reformation.

Martin Luther and his Protestant reforms made the Roman Catholics anxious about their Church. In 1545 a great Council of senior Catholic officials was set up at Trent, in northern Italy, and sat (with some breaks) until 1563. It had two purposes: to get rid of many slack practices of the Catholic Church, which Luther had rightly criticized, and to set down clearly the teachings of the Church. This painting shows the Council. On the right churchmen sit in dark rows. On the left, in red mantles and hats, are several cardinals, next to the pope the highest officials of the Catholic Church.

caught doing so. Some of the quarrels between Catholics and Protestants in Europe have lingered until modern times. But in most places these different types of Christian have learned to live together in peace.

The fall of Rome

In 1527 Rome was captured by an army containing many German followers of Luther. Some of them insulted and threatened senior Catholic churchmen. Nuns were captured and sold by the troops. And one German soldier showed what he thought of Renaissance culture by scratching the name of Martin Luther over a famous painting by Raphael.

Many Catholics in Italy were shocked by the temporary capture of Rome, and the spread of Protestantism in northern Europe. They were anxious to prevent the Catholic Church becoming any weaker. They opposed the ideas of Luther in many ways, but like him they despised the scholars of the Renaissance, who respected ancient pagan writers. These anxious Catholics no longer

allowed scholars and scientists in Italy the same freedom to express their views. Books containing Protestant or pagan ideas were banned by the Church. Only Catholics were allowed to receive degrees from Italian universities. It became far more difficult for people to teach and learn non-religious subjects. This strong Catholic reaction to the Reformation is

The sack of Rome in 1527. German and Spanish troops, fighting for the Holy Roman Emperor, capture the city.

CAPTA VRBE, ADRIANI PRAECELSA IN MOLE TENETVR
OBSESSVS CLEMENS, MVLTO TANDEM AERE REDEMPTVS.

called the Counter-Reformation. In Spain it frequently led to the torture of people believed not to be true Catholics.

The Italian decline

The Renaissance in Italy was dying. This was caused partly by the Counter-Reformation, and partly by the decline in Italian prosperity. In the 16th century Spain acquired huge amounts of silver and gold from its new American territories. This wealth helped to increase the power of Spanish traders in the western Mediterranean. Italian traders there found themselves making less and less profit. In the eastern Mediterranean Italian merchants had similar setbacks. The growth of a great Turkish empire there, in the late 16th century, prevented Italian traders from operating in many eastern areas. The wealth in Italy, which had supported the work of architects and sculptors, painters and scholars, was disappearing.

In parts of northern Europe, however, the traditions of the Renaissance lived on. Scientists there developed the theories created by Italians such as Galileo. Ancient Greek was studied in northern Europe, and it is still studied more there than anywhere else in the world. The pocket editions of books produced by Aldus Manutius were copied and became the forerunners of the modern small book. Architecture of the

A portrait of Erasmus by Hans Holbein the Younger, painted in 1523. Erasmus came from Rotterdam in the Netherlands. In Italy he studied the writings of Ancient Greek and Roman authors, and learned to write Latin perfectly. Erasmus was a Catholic, but he criticized the Church. During the Counter-Reformation Catholics were forbidden to read the books Erasmus had written because of this criticism, and because of his interest in the ancient pagan world.

Italian Renaissance was imitated for centuries, both in America and Europe. When the architect Christopher Wren designed the great Protestant cathedral of St. Paul's in London, in the late 17th century, he had in mind the Renaissance plan of St. Peter's in Rome. The classically inspired style of painting, which Renaissance artists had achieved, was developed by the superb 17th-century artists of the Netherlands and Flanders, and has never been lost. Before the Renaissance died out in Italy, it had helped to lay the foundations of our modern world.

Chiswick House, near London, designed by Lord Burlington in the "Palladian" style in about 1725. Lord Burlington traveled to Italy and admired the villas built by the 16th-century Italian architect Andrea Palladio. Palladio, in his turn, had admired the buildings of Ancient Rome! Many architects studied his villas closely and followed his ideas in some of their finest houses, especially in England.

Glossary

Renaissance artists gradually turned away from the Byzantine style of painting. This was a traditional style in which people were often painted against flat, gold backgrounds. They were shown wearing clothes with long narrow folds which formed patterns. People were not always copied from life. The infant Christ here does not have a large head like a real baby. Instead he is shown as a small adult. This picture of the Madonna and Child was painted by the 13th-century artist Cimabue in a style very close to Byzantine art.

Alliance An agreement to work or fight together. When two Italian cities quarreled over trade or the control of smaller neighbors, one city could often win by persuading a third city to help it against its rival. Such alliances were short-lived; today's friend might be tomorrow's enemy.

Arsenal A place where arms are made or stored. The original Arsenal was the shipyard set up by Venice to ensure that it always had ships for war and trade. It was so efficient that a warship could be equipped in hours.

Byzantine Empire Remains of the Eastern Roman Empire which by the 15th century had shrunk to the city of Constantinople (Byzantium). Before Renaissance times artists were much influenced by Byzantine art.

Charities Organizations which help the poor, the sick, the old, and orphans by giving them shelter or money. The Church and groups of laymen helped the needy; it was

considered a Christian duty but, except in Venice, the State did little.

Chastity Catholic priests, monks, and nuns promise not to marry or to have children. Sometimes in Renaissance Italy these vows of chastity were broken even by the pope, and there were scandals which helped to cause the Reformation.

Condottiere A general who hired himself and his troops to fight for a city. Some condottieri were among the best soldiers of the time, but sometimes they would change sides if paid enough, or even conquer and rule the cities they were hired to defend.

Counter-Reformation The attempt by the Church to end the spread of Protestantism by stopping the abuses which caused it. The Church also crushed freedom of thought by imprisoning thinkers like Galileo. Churchmen were afraid that bold thinkers might criticize the Church's ideas.

Courtier A relative or friend of a ruler who lived in the palace. Polite and clever courtiers made a ruler's life enjoyable. They were expected to be brave soldiers and skilled at languages, music, and poetry.

Crusades Military expeditions which in the Middle Ages set out from western Europe to capture the Holy Land and make it safe for Christian pilgrims.

Democratic government Form of government in which most of the people have a say. This was rare in Renaissance Italy. Some cities, like Milan, were ruled by one man; others, like Florence or Venice, by a few families.

Dowry Gift of money, land, or goods made by the bride's family to the groom. Among nobles and merchants, marriages were arranged to set up an alliance between families rather than to make the bride happy; the dowry was part of the contract.

Excommunication Anyone who disobeyed the Church could be deprived of the right to be forgiven his sins or receive Christian burial. If he died without being pardoned it was thought he would go to Hell. If a ruler was excommunicated, his subjects were excommunicated as well, unless they rebelled against him. The threat of excommunication was usually enough to make people submit to the pope.

Feud A long-standing and bitter quarrel between families. In Renaissance Italy a feud could lead to a vendetta – a series of revenge killings. These quarrels might be over money or politics.

The Florentine artist Uccello was so interested in perspective that he drew this careful diagram of a drinking cup to show its many different curves.

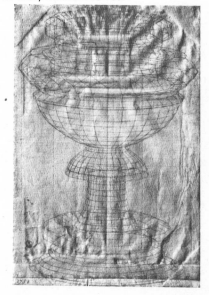

Florence A powerful city in north central Italy. Florence was supposed to be a republic but was controlled for much of the Renaissance by the Medici family. Many famous writers and artists, among them Dante and Michelangelo, were Florentines (as people who lived in Florence were known).

Lease An arrangement to pay for the use of someone's land. Italian peasants would often pay their landlords with a share of the crops. Leases were sometimes for very short periods, even as little as three years.

Middle Ages A name given to the centuries before the Renaissance. There is no definite agreement as to what period it covers. Some people consider that the Middle Ages start after the fall of Rome in AD 476; others consider the first few centuries after that date to be the "Dark Ages". There is no firm date for the end of the Middle Ages, either, since the Renaissance had no obvious beginning but grew up over many years.

Perspective Technique of painting scenes so that they appear to have depth and solidity, unlike the flat appearance of most earlier paintings. Renaissance painters noticed that distant objects appeared smaller; Brunelleschi noticed that parallel lines seem closer together as they get farther away.

Philosophy Study of how ideas and words describe – or fail to describe – the real world. In the Middle Ages, thinkers were concerned with the relationship between Man and the Christian God. In the Renaissance they were interested in the writings of the pagan Greek philosophers like Plato.

Pope Bishop of Rome and head of the Roman Catholic Church. In the Renaissance he ruled the Papal States, a large area of central Italy. Arguments over who should become pope weakened the Papacy.

Renaissance artists believed that art should follow mathematical rules. These rules were based on the art of Ancient Greece and Rome. In this drawing Leonardo da Vinci shows how the well-proportioned man, in different positions, can be fitted into "perfect" mathematical shapes such as the circle and the square.

Proportion The exact relationship between the size of an object and the size of its parts.

Protestant A western Christian who does not acknowledge the pope as his spiritual leader and instead follows the ideas of the Reformation.

Reformation In the early 16th century Martin Luther led a movement, called the Reformation, which objected to the misbehavior of the popes and of many churchmen. He wanted a simpler Christianity relying on faith and the study of the Bible instead of on ceremonies and tradition. The Protestant Reformation spread quickly through much of Northern Europe.

Renaissance The rediscovery of Ancient Greek and Roman ideas and skills, and the growth of art, trade and learning, were thought to be a rebirth of the ancient world rather than something new. "Renaissance" means "rebirth".

Roman Catholics Christians who recognize the pope as their spiritual leader – unlike the Protestant Churches, and the Orthodox Churches in Greece and Russia.

Serfs Country people who were forced to work for the landowner and could not move away. Serfs were not slaves since they could own things and were not themselves owned, but they were often unhappy and willing to rebel.

This glazed terracotta sculpture of the Madonna and Child was made by the della Robbia workshop in Florence in the early 16th century.

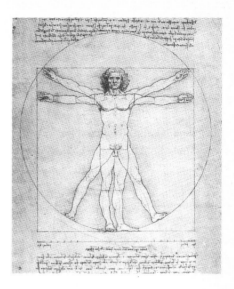

Techniques Ways of doing things. Italian painters discovered new ways of showing scenes in perspective and proportion.

Terracotta Clay which has been shaped and baked hard. It may be glazed, in order to decorate or make it watertight, or unglazed.

Venice The richest, most powerful city in northeast Italy. Venice was built on small coastal islands by people wanting protection from invaders. It became rich by trade. Perhaps the most famous Venetian was Marco Polo.

Index

Bold entries indicate a major mention.
Italic numerals indicate an illustration.

*paintings are reproduced throughout the book and text entries only are indexed

---

ACKNOWLEDGEMENTS

Photographs: Half title Scala, Milan/Baptistery, Florence; contents page, Scala, Milan/Duomo, Florence (top), Michael Holford (center), Scala, Milan/Uffizi, Florence (bottom); page 7 Scala, Milan/Loggia dei Lanzi, Florence (top), Scala Milan/Palazzo Ducale, Mantua (bottom); 8 Michael Holford; 10 National Gallery of Art, Washington (top), Museo Correr, Venice (bottom left), Scala, Milan/Palazzo Ducale, Venice; 11 Scala, Milan/Museo di Firenze com'era (top), National Gallery, London (bottom); 12 Mansell Collection (top), Scala, Milan/S. Apollonia, Florence; 13 Scala, Milan/S. Antonio, Padua; 14 Scala, Milan/Uffizi, Florence (top), Scala, Milan/Accademia, Florence (bottom); 15 Mansell Collection (top), Scala, Milan/Accademia, Venice (bottom); 18 Scala, Milan/Museo Correr, Venice (top), Scala, Milan/Castello del Buonconsiglio, Trent (bottom); 19 Mansell Collection (top), Scala, Milan/Palazzo Vecchio, Florence (bottom); 20 Scala, Milan/Museo Argenti, Florence (top); 21 British Museum (top), Scala, Milan (bottom); 22 Mary Evans (top), Louvre, Paris (bottom); 23 Scala, Milan/Brera Pinacoteca, Milan; 24 Picturepoint (top), Scala, Milan/Cappella de' Pazzi, Florence (bottom left), Scala, Milan/Accademia, Florence (bottom right); 25 Scala, Milan/Cappella Brancacci, S. Maria del Carmine, Florence; 26 Louvre, Paris (top), Scala, Milan/Uffizi, Florence (bottom); 27 Scala, Milan/Uffizi, Florence (top), Kunsthistorisches Museum, Vienna (bottom); 28 Scala, Milan/Duomo, Florence (top), St Bride Institute, London (bottom); 29 St Bride Institute, London (top), National Gallery, London (bottom); 30 Scala, Milan/Museo dell'Angelico, (top); 32 Scala Milan (top), Mansell Collection (bottom); 33 Rijksmuseum, Amsterdam (top), Victoria & Albert Museum, London (bottom); 34 National Gallery, London (top), Mansell Collection (bottom); 35 reproduced by gracious permission of Her Majesty the Queen, Royal Library, Windsor (top), Science Museum, London (center), Scala, Milan/Biblioteca Reale, Turin (bottom left), Scala, Milan/Gabinetto Disegni (bottom right); 36 Scala, Milan/S. Francesco, Assisi; 37 British Museum (top), Scala, Milan/Capodimonte, Naples; 38 British Museum (top), Michael Holford (bottom); 39 Mansell Collection; 40 Scala, Milan/S. Maria Maggiore, Trent (top), J. Powell (bottom); 41 Louvre, Paris (top), Architectural Association, London (bottom); 42 Louvre, Paris (top), Mansell Collection (bottom); 43 Mansell Collection (top), Christie, Manson & Woods Ltd, London (bottom).

Picture research : Jackie Cookson

AD 1250	*ITALY*	*EUROPE*

1250   **AD**

ITALY

1250–1494 Italy is split up into many different states. Florence, Venice, and Milan gain in wealth and power

1306 Giotto completes series of frescoes in Padua
1307 Dante Alighieri begins to write the *Divine Comedy*

1341 Francesco Petrarch crowned Poet Laureate, Rome
1348 Black Death ravages Italy and the rest of Europe

1400

1397 Medici bank is founded in Florence
1402 Ghiberti wins competition for the Baptistery doors, Florence

1420 Brunelleschi begins to build his dome for Florence Cathedral

1490 Aldus Manutius sets up Aldine press at Venice

1494–1559 France and Spain invade disunited Italy
1498 Savonarola burned at the stake

1500

1504 Michelangelo completes his statue of David

1527 Sack of Rome by Holy Roman Emperor

1559 Treaty of Cateau-Cambrésis. Habsburg Spain established as dominant power in Italy

EUROPE

1248–1270 Seventh Crusade led by Louis IX of France

1338 Beginning of Hundred Years' War (ends 1453)

1348 Black Death ravages Europe (until 1351)

1415 Henry V of England invades France and defeats French at Agincourt

1431 Jeanne d'Arc burned as a witch

1454 Printing by movable type perfected in Germany by Johannes Gutenberg
1456 Turks capture Athens

1492 Muslims expelled from Granada (Spain)

1517 Reformation begins: Martin Luther nails "protests" on church door at Wittenberg
1521 Diet of Worms: Martin Luther is condemned as a heretic and is excommunicated
1532 Religious Peace of Nuremberg: Protestants allowed to practice their religion freely
1545 Pope Paul III opens the Council of Trent which is to reform the Roman Catholic Church

NEAR EAST

ELSEWHERE

1260 Mamluk Turks control Egypt and Syria

1291 Saracens (Muslims) capture Acre from Christians

1301 Osman defeats Byzantines

1271–1275 Marco Polo, the Venetian explorer, travels to Cathay (China)

1294 Death of Kublai Khan

1363 Timur the Lame begins conquest of Asia

1368 Ming Dynasty in China (to 1644)

1379 Timur the Lame (Tamerlane) invades Persia

1390 Turks conquer Asia Minor

1402 Timur the Lame completes conquest of most of Ottoman empire

1421 Peking becomes capital of China

1400

1451 Mehemmed II becomes Sultan of Turkey

1453 Ottoman Turks capture Constantinople (Byzantium): end of the Byzantine empire and of the Middle Ages

1472 Venetians destroy Smyrna

1475 Turks conquer Crimea

1455 West Africa explored by the Venetian Cadamosto

1467 Start of civil wars in Japan

1492 Christopher Columbus discovers the New World

1497 John Cabot discovers Newfoundland

1498 Vasco da Gama of Portugal reaches India

1501 Amerigo Vespucci explores coast of Brazil

1513 Portuguese reach Canton, China

1517 Ottoman Turks capture Cairo; end of Mamluk empire

1522 First circumnavigation of the world by Magellan's expedition

1526 Mughal empire founded

1500

1520 Suleiman the Magnificent of Turkey begins 46-year reign

1549 St Francis Xavier introduces Christianity to Japan

1554 Turks conquer coast of North Africa

1557 Portuguese settle at Macao, China

1559